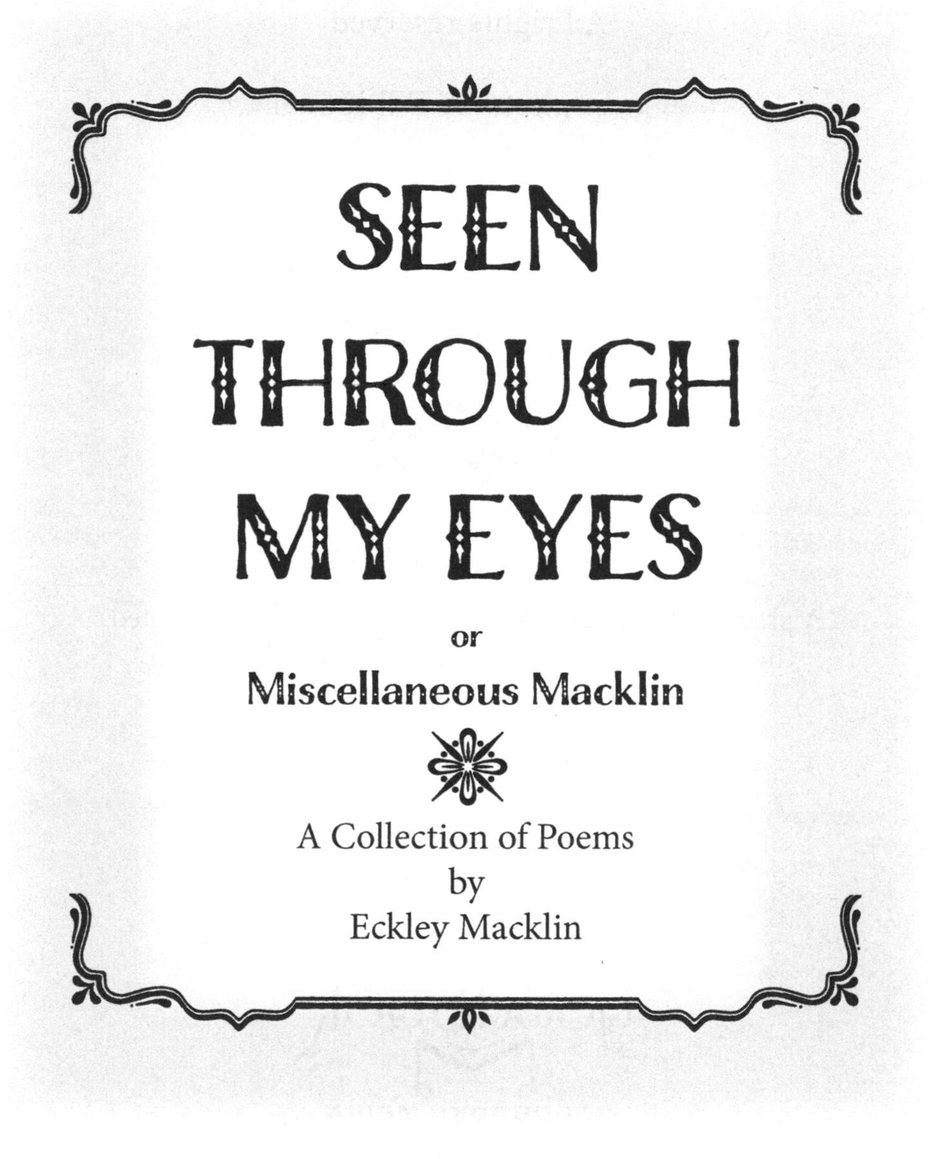

SEEN THROUGH MY EYES

or

Miscellaneous Macklin

A Collection of Poems
by
Eckley Macklin

Seen Through My Eyes

Cover photo by Bill Kainer
Book design by Jim Ridley
Published by Goodbooks Media

ISBN-13: 978-1512290936
ISBN-10: 1512290939

Printed in the USA

A previous limited edition of this collection was printed
in 1998 in Benque Viejo, Belize, Central America

Ad Majorem Dei Gloriam

GOODBOOKS MEDIA

3453 Aransas
Corpus Christi, Texas, 78411
goodbooksmedia.com

Table of Contents

Dedicated to my mother,
the true poet in my family

Introduction

n my dreams I return often to Elwood Street, which exists now only in the dreams and memories of those who lived there. It was there that I was born and it was there that my first poem was born early one sunny morning when I was nine years old.

I must have awakened later than usual on that particular day. My mother was already in the kitchen preparing breakfast and I was struck by the intense brilliance of the sunlight streaming through the bedroom windows. The almost mystical emotion which came over me would not leave me and I lay there, the simple but persistant words beating on my mind, until the composition in word and melody was complete and firmly impressed in my head forever. It was only then that I sat up on the bed and called out excitedly to my mother, "Ma, Ma, I just wrote a song!"

My First Poem

What a sunny day it was
With the sun so bright above,
And the children all at play
On that summer's day.
What a sunny day it was
With the birds singing all around
What a sunny day it was
In that old Virginia town.

The Boy on the Plow

he boy sat upon the plow, thinking boy thoughts, dreaming boy dreams. He had lived nine years on Earth. He had played upon its varied surface. He had come to love its fertile depth. And though he did not know life long, he had come to know life well. There were other things he could be doing, but, just sitting there tn that space, at that moment was what he should be doing, that and nothing more. The early summer sun was what he should be feeling; the rows of glowing corn he should be watching. In some other place he would have missed the dragonfly that darted 'cross the pond. He would not have seen the water strider's gliding streak. This was the first full day of summer with many summer days to come. But, there would never be another day like this: A day to sit upon the plow and think boy thoughts and dream boy dreams.

The Boy Looks at Twilight

Twilight 1s the worst time of day for little boys. Twilight, when daytime and playtime is over. Although the coming of night fascinated him, as he searched for the first star or the flicker of the first firefly and listened for the choir of frogs and the insect songs to come alive. The gray of dusk now made him feel a touch of sadness. The day was gone and the night was swiftly coming. But, would the daylight ever come again? Just because it came today did not mean that it would come tomorrow. The shadows in the distance came closer until they touched him, and he became one with them. The shadows were cool. He sat in the coolness and the darkness a little while more, until he heard his name being called from within the warm and well lit house, which stood just an arm's length away.

The Albizzia Tree

ne day I decided to build a village. I built it beneath the albizzia tree. Its feather-like leaves and soft pink flowers would be a paradise for my people living there. Out of bricks and bits of brick I built their one room homes. The roofs were made of sticks and other flat things lying in the yard. And then I made my people, created them from the cobs of corn and clothed them in the finest linen scraps my grandmother had tossed aside. I gave them hair of corn silk, golden and straight and tied around with a headband of thread. How handsome and beautiful they looked, my people. How proud I was to see them standing there, my own creation, product of my hand. And then I decided they must have a car to drive around the yard, scattering the chickens and ducks and geese, the dogs chasing and nipping at the tires. A large Diamond matchbox would be their coupe and a string would be the engine, powered by me, as I dashed around the yard and they followed obediently. In the evening I placed them inside of their strong and safe brick homes, and I too retired to the light of the lamp and the comfort of the family room. Then, like a god watching over his creation at night, from the window I would look at the spot where my little village stood and hope that my people were happy and warm in their village beneath the albizzia tree.

The Girl with the Long, Red Pigtails

hey came running across the field, calling his name;
his cousin and the girl with the long red pigtails.
Why did they bother him here?
This was his place, his refuge:
the tree beside the ditch in the middle of the field.
It was a peach tree and the first day he found it
the fruit was green and hard and he had returned
each day, waiting for the first, faint blush of pink,
showing soon it would be red and soft and ripe.
He could wait.
He could wait all summer.
He had no place to go and the tree, his tree would
always be there.
But now this girl, this girl with the long, red pigrails,
the freckles and the big front teeth had found him.
Why had his cousin done this?
Didn't she know he liked to be alone here with
his tree, his thoughts, his solitude?
He would not talk.
He would not be friendly.
But, they ran back across the field, smiling and
laughing just as they had come.
The girl came twice more that summer.
He acted much the same, but he was beginning to like it when
he saw the two of them come racing across the field.

He liked to see the pigtails as they bounced upon her shouders.
Her smile he could see in the distance, the sound of her voice calling his name — and then she came no more.
The summer days that before had come and gone so swiftly now grew longer and longer as he looked across the fields, waiting, hoping.
One day before the end of summer his cousin took him to the girl 's house.
He could not take his eyes from her.
She was so beautiful.
There, she was the one who looked shy.
"We are moving to the North," her mother told him.
"When?" He could hardly get it out.
"Before the start of school." Like an echo in his mind these words seemed to come from a great, great distance. His knees became weak. He leaned against the window and held back the tears that wished to flow.
He never returned to the tree to see the peach grow ripe.
It was no longer his alone.
It belonged to them.
He would never love again, he knew.
How could he?
He no longer had a heart.
His heart had gone with her, with the freckles and the long, red pigtails whom he would never, ever see again.

Southern Sunday

Out of bed early and down the stairs
Then down on our knees for morning prayers.

With one eye closed and one eye looking,
Smelling bacon in the kitchen cooking,

After a hymn and a Bible verse
Giving praise to the saints and to sinners a curse,

We breakfast on biscuits and scrambled eggs
Happily swinging our little legs.

Our heads now brushed, our faces washed clean
And rubbed down with a little bit of Vasoline.

We start down the lane to the Baptist church
Going through groves of live oak and birch.

Down the main road for about a mile
We pass by others with a nod and a smile.

There's Nellie May with her head held high
Looking like her nose is going to suck up the sky.

The young ones begin with Sunday School
Learning about Jesus and the Golden Rule.

Then about noon the preacher begins
Reminding us all about our daily sins.

The preacher starts soft but he ends up loud,
Whipping up the Holy Ghost in the crowd.

Some folks begin to shout Amen.
Heads in the choir begin to roll and spin.

Old Miz Fannie lets out a shout
And the bench begins to shake 'cause she's big and stout.

And I just sit there wonderin'
When is all of this stuff about to end?

In spite of the fact that we had to pray
And stay in the church nearly all the day,

Sunday was still the best day of the week
Because of all the great things we got to eat:

Chicken and ham and fresh made rolls,
Corn on the cob and greens filling bowls,

Sweet potato pie, ice cream home made
All washed down with cold lemonade.

Oh, to live those days just one more time
I'd give my whole fortune, I'd give my last dime.

The Country Store

The little brown boy stood all alone
Waiting to be served so he could go home.
His gramma had sent him to the country store
For a bag full of flour and nothing more.
Maybe she wanted to bake him a pie.
Now, he stood silent as clerks passed him by.
Is it because I'm so small that they can't see?
Those white, grown-up people came in long after me.
He knew the true answer and that's why it hurt.
He was a small boy, not a pile of brown dirt.
And then, when the last man had gone out the door,
The clerk looked at him, standing down on the floor.
"What do you want, boy?", he finally said
To the child whose spirit was now almost dead.
The boy somehow made the words come out
In a whisper, although he wanted to shout.
"My gramma sent me for some flour, sir,"
As promptings to hatred began to stir.
But, his mother had taught him to hate no one
And he had tried to be an obedient son.
He was hurt, but the pain would soon go away
And he had more playing to do that day.
Poor little boy! If he were so clever
He'd had known that the pain would go on forever.

With troubled heart, he returned to the farm
And placed the bag in his grandmother's arm.
"Gramma, ask me to do any chore,
But, please, don't send me to that place no more."

My Street

One morning I went out to sit on the steps
On the front of my house. I was feeling
A bit alone but I was used to that
And liked it that way on my street.
It was quiet as it often was. Few cars
Passed this way and no-one was walking.
Suddenly, a door across the street was opened
And out came a boy my age who sat on the steps
Of a house across the street.
Where did he come from? How did he
Get here? Who had invited him to my
Street? It seemed to me we sat there for hours,
Although it was only for minutes,
As I felt the sense of being
Threatened swell up inside.
Yet he never looked my way.
Purposely, it seemed, he kept his
Face turned toward the corner
As if I were just not there.
In a little while he stood up
And went inside without a glance
In my direction. How dare, I thought,
He ignore me on my street. All of
That day I was angry. I'll show him
If he crosses the street to this
Side. This is my street, not his. On
The next day in the morning I went

Out again and sat on the steps and
Waited and waited, but, he never
Appeared and, after a while, I got
Tired and went back in. Maybe
He moved, I thought, and was only
Here for a day. I was glad he was
Gone but somehow I missed him.
I wondered who he was and how he
Was related to the people across the
Street. On the third day I went
Out again. I had almost forgotten
The boy. But then his door opened
And he came out and sat on his steps.
He looked down the street one way
And he looked down the street the
Other way, but he never looked
At me. After a while he got up
And stood for a moment or two.
He started to move to the
Sidewalk and then to the curb.
He started across the street
Toward me. I stood up with my
Hands balled up in fists behind my back.
I'll show him, I said to myself; I'll
Show him. When he came up to me,
He said, "Want to be friends?"
"Yes," I said, and we were.

My Voice Doesn't Sing Anymore

"My voice doesn't sing anymore," my mother said
one day in sadness and I, too, felt the same,
remembering how I loved to hear her sing when
I was young. The memories filled my mind.
"Rock-a-bye baby in the tree top," I hear;
her face smiling down on me, as I, for sure,
smiled back. She had a song for each of us:
A song for me, one for my brother, one for my
father and a song of her own. "Moonlight
becomes you .... ": A beautiful song for a
beautiful mother. And she could sing in
harmony with melodies that came across the air.
That, I found a marvelous thing, not knowing how
such a wondrous feat was done. Year after year
she sang and then she sang no more. One day
not long ago I heard her start a song and just
as quickly stop. The notes had become too
high. "My voice doesn't sing anymore," she
said. If your voice will not sing, then hum,
My dear, please hum.

Eula

I have tried to remember the first time I was aware of her presence. I cannot. It seems that she was always there. She was not too tall and not too short, always slight in figure. Her complexion medium brown, her head topped by graying, never gray but always graying hair. Sometimes she would loosen the braids she wore and let her hair down to comb and brush. I marveled at its length and how soft it looked. She must have been a handsome woman when young but I never saw her young. She was Gramma.

My Father Died at Eighty-three

My father died at eighty-three
When I was fifty-seven.
While I was stranded on the earth
My father flew to Heaven.

Eckley, PA

I once took a trip down to Eckley, PA,
This town that was named after me.
East of the interstate, not out of the way
Going south to the southern valley.

I first saw the town in the afternoon sun,
Its day in the sun then long past.
Clearly, the work of the town was now done.
In shadows, how long could it last?

Built for the men who worked in the mines,
Named for a benefactor's son,
It saw its good days and had its hard times
Until all the mining was done.

Facing sure death, the town would not die;
Changed by time, but alive.
A monument standing where dead men now lie
Awaiting their time to revive.

A few years ago I'd have changed that good name,
But now I can claim it with pride.
While neither of us will ever know fame,
I know that the name will survive.

Kissing Cousins

They knew it was wrong:
So close of kin,
Where a mere embrace
Might seem a sin.

What could they do?
So deep entwined,
Yet, forbiddened the path
With roses lined.

How oft it was
Longing eyes would meet;
But, fearful hearts
Shrank in retreat.

For God in heaven
Had deemed it so:
Cousins only kiss
And then let go.

Storm

Amid dark waves and wintry frost
A ship was windswept, broken, lost.
'Twas lost, 'twas lost within the cloud;
A dead soul draped in vail and shroud.

The firmament hurled forth its wrath
Forcing the ship from chartered path.
Her destiny was sealed in doom;
A watery grave to be her tomb.

No aid was sought for from on high.
"Why worship we an empty sky?"
Then, from the depth of deep despair
One voice was lifted up in prayer.

"0, Father, Creator, 0 Guiding Power,
Have mercy, mercy in this hour."
One mighty plea by angels flown
From Earth's dark sea to Heaven's throne.

Now from the death that stalked her floor
The keel turned toward the distant shore.
Sail on! Sail on! 0 sails beloved
By forces sent down from above.

From out of the midst of that frothing sea
Sailed forth the vessel "Victory".
No tempest followed in her wake
For God was the captain in charge of her fate.

The Curtain of Night

The curtain of night has drawn away
Revealing the soft gray mist of day.
The first ray steals through waiting trees;
The forest wakes as long night flees.

The dew drops, sparkling in the sun
Like gems, adorn the day begun.
The beauty of the waking hour
Reflects in each fair, flaming flower.

A cock now crows to herald morn;
A page of the book of time is born.
With songs on wing, the birds on high
Give greeting to the morning sky.

And man, too, like the bird and beast,
Can celebrate the morning feast.
We need not long in darkness grope.
Awake! Morning is the hour of hope.

Seen Through My Eyes

Seen through my eyes
Most men are either good or misguided,
On the right trail or confused.
And, whether I'm praised or derided,
My soul remains light and amused.

Seen through my eyes
Most days are clear and quite sunny
And morning brings buckets of dew.
If my eggs are cooked hard or still runny,
It is breakfast, so why should I rue?

Seen through my eyes
Most clouds do not last long:
Swiftly they pass through the sky.
Rather than crying, I keep singing this song,
“I'm going to live till the day that I die."

Why should I fret and why should I worry?
Things either were, are, or to be.
Whether I'm slow or in a big hurry,
Time will move on without me.
Seen through my eyes.

Many An Evening

Many an evening I have spent
Listening to the rhythms sent
By a hundred peepers as they rent
The air with piping 'cross a springtime pond.

So, often on an autumn night
As I watched the wild geese in their flight,
I sensed my ear was turned aright
To the plaintive honking of their one-note song.

On hidden lakes I've heard the loon;
While in the Tundra's wintry gloom
The lonely wolves sing to the moon,
Not knowing that their notes would go that far.

For all of nature is a song:
A melody great ages long,
Sung by a choir a billion strong
In harmonies that ring from star to star.

This is the music of the spheres
Which every watching angel hears
(Although it's silent to our ears),
As it peals forth from heaven's concert hall.

Still, we can hear the endless beat
Of crashing cymbals that repeat
When waves upon the shoreline leap
In answer to the ancient Siren's call.

The roll of thunder's mighty drum,
Before the tinkling raindrops come,
We hear. We hear the soft winds hum
Or whistle when the tree tops reel and rock.

Once at a concert in the park,
As the hills to the west were turning dark,
Above the flutes I heard a lark,
And in that moment knew the birds sing Bach.

Luke 12: 22-30

See the lilies of the field,
How they spin and labor not.
Even kings in royal attire
To their glory cannot aspire.
Yet, the flowers last but a day.
By tomorrow they are gone away.

We hear ravens everywhere.
They do not sow and do not reap.
They do not store their grain in barns
And safely hide from wind and storms.
Someone listens when ravens call.
He even knows when sparrows fall.

For men and nations the same is true:
That God in heaven provides for you.
So do not worry and do not care
What you will eat, what you will wear.
Only those whose faith is weak
Do not believe the words I speak.

Haiku

The seed makes its way
Pushed by wind, carried by rain
Into the earth's heart.

Ripples on water
Tell me that something touched it
And sank to its soul.

I hear the rain fall
On the roof and get shivers
From the cooling sound.

I hear a horned owl
Sing its plaintive song far off
As the night draws near.

Birds sing at daybreak,
So why should I not join them
With my song of joy?

The days of summer
End now in one grand burst of
Searing radiance.

Joy is forever.
Pain, lasting a moment here,
Dies with the body.

The Smallest Maple Tree

Today I took
a rest beneath
the smallest maple tree.
It did not have much shade, but it
was just enough for me.
Its leaves were much more closely packed
than those of greater height,
And sunshine could not make it through
pushing with all its might.
Big trees have their jobs to do
and each one does its part.
The small trees
cannot do
as much
but try
with all
their heart.

After the Rain

The summer evening rain has stopped
and the world is changing colors.
The grey, the pink, the orange tinted clouds
break and melt into the freshened sky,
which hid behind the rumbling hills
raindrops ago.

From sheltering boughs, the birds appear
and twitter night songs on their
high pole perch while one half rainbow's
shining droplets slip away and purple
puddles mirror the final, dying
sparks of day.

I Watch the Evening

I watch the
Evening lest it slip away without warning,
Without sound, sneaking down the sky
To some unknown hiding place
Leaving me alone and
In darkness waiting
For the
Dawn.

Seasons

Wintry
winds
from
now
on
I
do
see
will
bring
spring.
Summer
turns
soon
for
me
a
so
far
away
balmy
autumn.

Perhaps

Perhaps the winter times came first
When all was dark and drear,
And the wind that blew through caves of ice
Was all that one could hear.

Perhaps snow crowned the entire world
From polar spar to keel,
And the cold that clung to frigid peaks
Was all that one could feel.

Perhaps not man nor beast was formed
And birds were yet to be,
And the barren ice fields' frozen waste
Was all that one could see.

Perhaps that's why the sun was born
And the seasons given birth.
Perhaps that's why from seeds came life
And spring came to the earth.

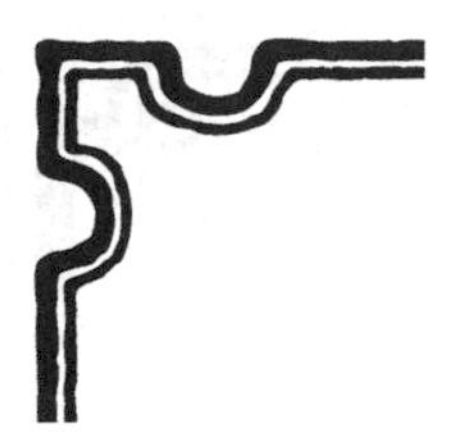

First Snow

Small droplets gathered in a cloud
Until there was a droplet crowd.

And droplets teetered on thc edge
Of the crowded, cloudy ledge.

Looking at the ground below,
They talked of who'd be first to go.

Someone standing near the rear
Shouted so that all could hear,

"The oldest should be first, for he
Would like to grow a giant tree."

"Not me," a voice was heard to scream.
"I want to fill a tiny stream."

They talked of who would be the showers
That sprinkled on the pretty flowers.

And on and on their voices rose
Till no one knew just whom they chose.

Now there came a cold north breeze
And droplets, fearing they might freeze,

In just one simple magic stroke
Were wrapped up in a soft white coat.

The ones behind began to shove
And snow flakes drifted from above.

While Camping by a Pond

The grass was wet beneath my feet
As I stepped out upon morning
And listened to the silent song:
The lilting hush upon the yet-still air.
And I breathed in morning deeply,
While it spread throughout my blood and bones
And rested on my face and limbs.
The morning star was sitting on the mist
That touched me with its wispy fingers;
But, calling me more loudly back was sleep,
For this was not my time as yet.
So, back into the tent I crept
Until the sun had chased the silent song,
The star, the misty fingers, and the sleep away.

While Camping by a Pond II

The grass was wet beneath my feet
As I stepped out on morning
And listened to the silent song:
The lilting hush of dawning.

The morning air was calm and still,
The glassy pond unshakened.
The morning star stood on the mist.
The birds had not yet wakened.

The mist touched me upon my face.
I felt its wispy fingers
As they passed before my eyes
Where remnant night still lingers.

Waiting for the sleeping sun
As the dew was falling,
Back into the tent I crept
Where a dream was calling.

Autumn Vista

Than this, I had not seen an autumn quite as bold.
One would have thought this was the last display
Of nature, decked in robes of glowing gold
Before the earth, in glory, passed away.

Vast fields of yellow grain sat at the feet
Of patchwork-quilted hills, upon whose lap
The autumn leaves were curling up in sleep
Soon after feeding on the breasted sap.

And, while I bundled up from head to heel,
Anticipating winter's icy flow,
Deep in my heart I could already feel
The dauntless seeds of spring begin to grow.

One Raindrop Fell

One raindrop fell.
But who took note?
It fell among ten thousand times ten thousand more.
And yet how blessed it was.
One fish breathed in its flowing life.
One man has quenched his aching thirst.
One seed has taken root.

One flower grew.
But who took note?
It grew among a thousand times a thousand more.
And yet, how blessed it was.
One bee sipped nectar from its cup.
One man inhaled its sweet perfume.
One seed has taken root.

One tree in the forest.
But who took note?
It stood among a hundred times a hundred more.
And yet, how blessed it was.
One bird has nested in its arms.
One man found rest within its shade.
One seed had taken root.

One gentle word.
But who took note?
It stood alone.
And yet how blessed it was.
One little face now wears a smile.
One man now walks with lighter step.
One seed has taken root.

At the Gathering of the Leaves

Talk of snow-filled branches shaking;
Talk of springtime buds awaking;
Talk of chill winds and frost heaves
At the gathering of the leaves.

Talk of robins who were nesting;
Talk of weary hikers resting;
Talk of hot days and warm eves
At the gathering of the leaves.

Talk of apple cider making;
Talk of pumpkin pies and baking;
Talk of patches, quilts and weaves
At the gathering of the leaves.

Talk of howdy-do and greeting;
Talk of good friends who are meeting;
Talk of rolling up our sleeves ·
At the gathering of the leaves.

Heat and Humidity

Man was not made to live in humidity.
The Garden of Eden was cool and quite dry.
We suffer today because of stupidity:
Stealing an apple to eat on the sly.

Soft fruit, like oranges, as far as could see
Were grown in the garden for mankind to munch.
But, not happy with that, Adam was greedily
Biting the one fruit that had a sharp crunch.

That is the story of why we are suffering;
For God, who was nearby, heard the loud noise
And caught Adam red handed, mouth full and stuttering,
In only his bearskin and lacking in poise.

Remembrance

Remembrance beats upon the
Shore of mind, its weathered
Grains slip out to sea and
Deeper sea leaving smooth
Where once were ripples on
The beach, the beach whose
Ends stretched out of sight
Around each bend at left and
Right.
And when I walked along
The beach I liked to look
Behind to see whence I had come
And progress made, each
Footprint's tale so clearly told
In shadow and in sun.
And when I walked as far as time
Allowed, turning to return, I saw
The tide had come and swept
Away all sign
That I had ever come that way.
Now who would ever know
The marks I made upon the shore?
Those who come tomorrow will
Make a fresh impression
Followed by their own remembrance.

Up the Nile

I want to go up the Nile.
I don't know why.
There is something that awaits me there.
I don't know what.
Is there a temple someplace overgrown with vines?
A temple that only I am permitted to find.
Is there a message carved on a hidden stone?
A message that tells me that I have come home.
Will my ears hear voices, dead long ago,
Reminding me of things that I used to know?
Will I feel a surge rush through my blood
As I cut through the bush and crawl through the mud?
Will my feet tread pathways from ages past
Till I come to a village I know at last?
Will ancestors, forefathers with arms open wide
Greet me and ask me to sit at their side?
Will my tongue taste food ancient markets once sold?
Will I sip new wine out of gourds that are old?
It makes little sense to go on with this.
I have never seen the Nile — although I crossed it once.

Teotihuacan

Dedicated to Luis Olmos, my friend and guide in Mexico.

I stand atop a pyramid in Mexico.
Those who built it are no longer here;
their names carved on no weathered stone.
The wind whispers past my ear, but it
carries not the slightest hint of voices
dead so long ago. Down below in plazas
once filled with men who spoke the
language of their day, I search for just
one sign, one footprint left from days
of kingdoms past, but all I find is dust
the years have piled upon their passing.
And what of you, my friend, sweating
over stones you carve for everlasting
praise? Carve on, if you will. You will
not find here what you seek. For
immortality you must look elsewhere.

In the Holy Land

The haze circles the mountain;
A calm covers the sea;
A songbird sings in the distance.
Dawn's horn is calling me.

Dewdrops gleam on bright petals;
Spring grass reflects the glow.
In the silent hush of morning
I hear a voice I know.

"Come, follow in my footsteps.
Come, tread the path I'll show.
Bread for the journey I'll give you
And wine for your cup will flow."

In the deserts of Judea,
Through the fields of Yizreel,
To the streets of old Jerusalem
I will sing, I will praise, I will kneel.

From Tabor's lofty summit
To the shores of Galilee,
I will walk together with Jesus
Who daily walks with me.

Rome Fell One Day

Rome fell one day.
Its strength could not last
On weakened foundations
Sunk deep in the past.

From Hittite to Persian:
Great Kingdoms of old,
Whose people were exiled
Into bondage or sold.

Babylon and Nineveh,
The sands will not tell
Where you hid in your vastness
On the day that you fell.

America, beloved,
Have you nothing to fear,
As your morals are shattered
And your bow starts to veer?

The prophets are speaking;
Listen to the voice
Of one who is pleading
"Make the right choice."

America, wake up!
Do you not hear the call?
Do you feel the earth tremble?
Why do you stall?

America, dear one,
Your future was bright,
But, while you were sleeping,
The day turned to night.

My country, arise!
The foe is at the gate.
Your days are now numbered,
But, it's still not too late.

Fools' Progress

We've got to make progress.
We can't fall behind.
The earth is a-moving,
And we're losing time.

Out with the old;
In with the new.
These things are red;
Let's paint them all blue.

Although we have cut this,
Let's cut it again.
We cannot make progress
Unless there is pain.

So snip a bit here
And clip a bit there.
Change things for change sake.
The message is clear.

Keep moving, keep changing,
For reason or whim.
This is our motto.
This is our hymn.

?

I
DO
NOT
KNOW
NOR
DO
I
DO
NOW
WHAT
YOU
DO
I
AM
NOT
WITH
YOU
AM
I
?

Call, Call into the Night

Call, call into the night,
Voice astride the wind;
Riding up the crested height
To the river's farthest bend.

Call, call into the night,
Casting all aside
To rush toward the distant light
And meet the coming bride.

Call, call into the night.
Sleeping love awakes
And joins with Eros in his flight
Until the new day breaks.

Prayer to a Poet

Oh, poet, do not spread before me the table of despair. Bring me the cup of love. Set before me the platter of beauty. Kindle for me one tiny spark of light, that having sipped one drop, tasted one morsel, discovered one path unseen before, I may with new life continue on my journey one more day. And I will take a little of you with me to share with another weary traveller whom I may meet along the way. And who knows with whom he may later share? Then, poet, you will have performed your duty well, and one more soul will give you thanks.

A Love Song

One note is the start of a love song.
One step begins a dance.
And the moment I saw you
I knew it was love in a glance.

A poem is not long in its telling.
The truth is but a word.
And when two lovers are speaking,
A sigh may be all that is heard.

One candle will banish the darkness.
One star will lead you home.
And just one thought of you, my love,
Is comfort when I am alone.

I Remember

I remember
Windsongs at the close of
the day.

I remember
How the trees would listen
and sway.

I remember
From the start

Lovely whispers
After dark,

When words deep
In my heart

I'd whisper to you.
My gift to you.

I remember
How the sky was colored
in blue.

I remember
In the morning grass filled
with dew.

I remember
All the while

Your laughter
Like a little child

And the funny
Little smile

You gave to me.
Your gift to me.

A Christmas Lullaby

Across snowfields where crystals grow,
Up starbanks where moonbeams glow,
Wee one searches to and fro
For the place where daydreams go.

Like a fledgling to its nest
Come, child, from thy distant quest.
Sleep o'er spreads thee with her charm
As I tuck thee in my arm.

While the gentle snowdrops fall
Down on rooftops, low and tall,
Back and forth the voices call
"Merry Christmas, one and all!"

Snowflakes

Snowflakes through the long night fall,
Whispering a silent call.
Calling as they twist and twirl
To each sleeping boy and girl.

One by one they touch the ground,
Softly, making not a sound.
See them sparkle, see them shine
Covering the firs and pine.

"Little children, come and play.
Run through snowdrops all the day."
Tiny footsteps in the snow
Show us where they come and go.

Riding snowsleds down the hill,
Boys and girls together spill.
Hear their happy shouts of glee
Echo from each snow filled tree.

Warm and snug in bed at night,
All their cares tucked out of sight.
Snowflakes swirling down in streams
Kiss them in their happy dreams.

One more joyful day now past,
The children safely home at last,
High above a distant hill
One child's star is twinkling still.

He Comes

He comes and I wait.
The soft footsteps I hear.
The sheep and cows grow restless.
I know that he is near.

He comes and I wait.
They will not let me in.
"Go change and wash thyself anew.
Thy soul is stained with sin."

I wash and I wait.
My soul and body gleam.
Then from a distant, ancient star
The angel voices stream.

He comes and I wait
Until the night is fair,
Then I will open the stable door
And find him waiting there.

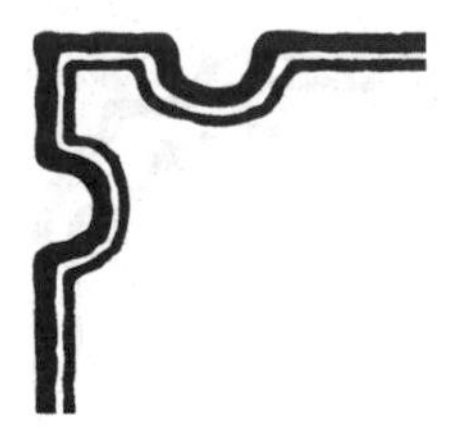

Evil Walks, Evil Talks

Evil walks the streets today,
Hawking out its sordid wear
Hour after hour.

Evil has a voice today:
Roaring like a hungry bear
Seeking to devour.

Evil can be seen today
Spread out on the table.
Many rush to choose it.

Evil stands in light of day
Where those who see are able
To refuse it.

Last Message to a Young Friend

When we are young with conscience free
Each day is filled with joy and glee.
And then temptations come along:
The strong choose right, the weak choose wrong.

Ah, sin, how very sweet it seems
When answering our deep, dark dreams.
Its chain entwines us link by link
As down into the mire we sink.

The world, which seemed a great bright way
Is slowly changed to barren clay.
Do not be captured in your youth.
Avoid all evil, walk with truth.

Young one, beware the gilded cup!
Eat not of Adam's fruit at sup!
Oh, you with ears that will not hear,
For you, I shed a final tear.

Contemplations

I have known great men I did not meet.
Have dreamt great dreams but without sleep.

I have been alone while in a crowd.
Have stood in rags but yet been proud.

I have lived long years yet died each day.
Have been at home though miles away.

I have loved mankind yet loved no one.
Have stood my ground yet dared to run.

I have had great treasures yet owned none.
Have never started yet been done.

I have listened yet I have not heard.
Have spoken yet not said a word.

I have shunned the world yet loved the earth.
Have been reborn without rebirth.

Questions and Answer

What did we have before we had flowers?
Why is there a rainbow right after it showers?
Who made the wind?
What makes it blow?
Where does wind come from?
Where does it go?
Why does the rain fall?
What makes it snow?
Why is water wet?
Why is fire hot?
Why is this true and why is this not?
Why is grass green?
Why is the sky blue?
Who made me?
Then who made you?

Those are good questions
But, before there's another,
Daddy is quite busy
So, please, ask your mother.

Invocation

Many a summer has come
and many a summer has gone,
Since I was a boy.
Yet, still, the boy lives on.
He will not leave.

Many a friend has come
and many a friend has gone,
Since I was a boy.
Some have departed in death.
And, thus, I grieve.

Through many cups of sadness,
through many feasts of joy,
You, God, were always there
With food to refresh,
With drink to relieve.

Mansion in Heaven

My brother has a mansion in heaven. Jesus told him so.
He always wanted a fine house here on Earth below.
But, fortune left him with one red cent,
In spite of the hours at work that he spent.
Such may have made another dispair,
But he accepted the fact that life was not fair.
Hard work was something he seemed to enjoy.
He took to it like a child to a toy.
He was never content to go home and rest
Until he was pleased he had given his best.
He was quiet and shy and never could boast,
Though he did many things much better than most.
Yet, the more his earthly fortune sank,
The more he stored up in his heavenly bank.
So, now he has a mansion above
And the greatest of treasures – his Father's love.

Notes

My Voice Doesn't Sing Anymore
Published in *Treasured Poems of America*
Winter 1992 edition by Sparrowgrass Poetry Forum

Seen Through My Eyes
Written in Nairobi (Karen) Kenya, April 7, 1997

Many An Evening
Published in *The Cord, A Franciscan Spiritual Review*,
Volune 33, No. 5 May, 1983

While Camping by a Pond
Published in *New Haven Journal-Courier*, 1969
Poetic Voices of America Spring 1992 edition
by Sparrowgrass Poetry Forum

Remembrance
Published in *Emily Dickinson, A Centennial Celebration*
(1890-1990) by Bristol Banner Books

Teotihuacan
Written in Puebla, Puebla Mexico July, 1993

In the Holy Land
Written in Galillee, Israel February 25, 1990

A Christmas Lullabye,
Snowflakes,
He Comes
Published in *Twelve for Christmas*
by Goodbooks Media, 2013

Made in the USA
Middletown, DE
27 March 2021